Mental health Billing from Claims Denied to NPIs

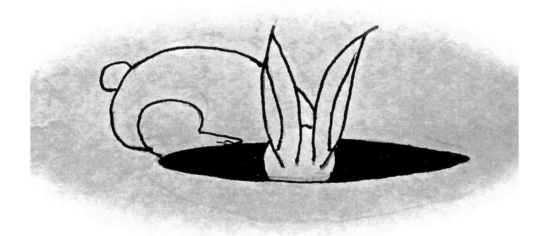

Tips for the Baffled, Bewildered, Befuddled Provider

Julie Rice, PsyD, LMFT

Dianne Hayward, EdM, MAC

AMAZON

Copyright 2014 - All rights reserved

Disclaimer

We make no guarantees regarding the accuracy or completeness of this book. Anything we forgot to add is covered. And guess what, the advice may not work for everyone. We are not liable for any loss of profit. This book is based on our personal experiences.

Acknowledgements

We want to thank Denise Armstrong, billing expert. She read our first draft and corrected our mistakes. Frankly, we were laughing so hard we needed a voice of reason.

TABLE OF CONTENTS

Preface 5

Introduction 9

Chapter 1 FIRST Things First 13

Chapter 2 WHAT is a Panel, a Network, a PPO, an HMO? 15

Chapter 3 CREDENTIALING 17

Chapter 4 THE Cryptic and Challenging CMS 1500 20

Chapter 5 CALLING Insurance Companies 29

Chapter 6 Claim Denied! Don't PANIC!! 41

Chapter 7 Keeping Track of Clients and Companies 47

Chapter 8 EAP Employee Assistance Program 51

Chapter 9 What is TRICARE and Why Should You Care? 53

Chapter 10 Medicare 57

Chapter 11 Out of the Rabbit Hole 60

Glossary 62

New Version CMS 1500 66

All the TIPS 67

Bibliography 70

Resources 70

Did you know?

- *Did you know insurance companies might contact you to get you to accept a lower fee than you originally contracted?*

- *Did you know that a patient's insurance policy and/or coverage can and does change in the middle of the year?*

- *Did you know that sometimes an out-of-network provider is paid at a higher rate than an in-network provider?*

- *Did you know that insurance companies buy each other out unexpectedly and then the names change?*

- *Did you know you might have to submit claims with organizations other than the original insurance company?*

- *Did you know working with insurance companies is equivalent to running with scissors?*

We have written this book because when we went looking for behavioral health insurance billing information it was very scarce. When we turned to the medical billing texts for information they were 700 pages long and 95% of the content didn't apply to mental health. In addition, the texts we did find were freaking boring.

We were even willing to take a course but really didn't want to spend a year in classes most of which we wouldn't need, learning information that wouldn't apply to the behavioral health field. We didn't need to memorize the codes for radical heart surgery, colonoscopy, etc. You get the idea.

We want to be very clear with you. We are NOT experts in insurance billing. As non-experts we have written this book so it will be understandable, informative, readable and most importantly FUN. We hope that our occasional irreverence will make this easier to absorb.

We are sharing our experiences as a service to others like us. We hope that the following information will guide you through your own adventure in behavioral health billing. We hope you will share information not included here because heaven knows we can use all the help we can get when going up against big insurance.

PREFACE

Ok, you are in private practice ready to work with your clients. How exciting! Initially, you may resist filing insurance claims because of the stories you have heard. FYI: They are true and your instinct makes perfect sense. BUT at some point, for financial reasons, you might give in and decide to work with insurance companies. They are a pain but according to Dr. Julie they are mostly worth it.

Here are our stories. DO NOT SKIP THE STORIES. Our stories are provided in order to illustrate the issues of interacting with big insurance companies.

Dr. Julie's Story

<u>A Heroic Journey into Insurance-World</u>

I am a Marriage and Family Therapist. Long, long ago, before I lost my innocence, I completed my Masters Program. I successfully passed the licensing exams. I opened my private practice with a light heart. Then I sat and sat and sat. It became evident that my extensive coursework had left out an important subject: how to make my practice lucrative. I soon discovered that private pay clients were not thick on the ground, in the air or anywhere else I could find. I realized I would have to plunge into the rabbit hole: the mysterious world of insurance billing.

I call it that because established therapists I knew shuddered when they talked about their experiences. They bemoaned the fact that the paperwork was impenetrable. They had trouble discovering whether a new client had a deductible, copay or limited sessions. Then they had to fill in the tangled web of the CMS 1500, turn it in, after which their claims were denied. They had to join panels, apply to be in-network, stay out-of-network, and know the difference between a PPO and an HMO.

In spite of their warnings, in the end I hoped for a financial benefit. I decided I was willing to travel into the Circles of Hell about which my peers had warned me.

In the beginning, a colleague, who was trying to help me out, gave me a sample CMS 1500 form, the mandated insurance billing form. When I saw all the small print, all those spaces to fill in, my eyes crossed and I felt nauseous. And even

If I could fill it out, what was I supposed to do with the blasted thing?

To answer that question, I had to inquire whether I submitted it by snail mail, online, fax, email, or by carrier pigeon to the insurance company. Now the fun part is that different insurance companies had different protocols for submitting the same CMS 1500 form and that was just the beginning of many frustrating interactions.

Somehow I blithered along until one day I realized that this business of dealing with insurance companies and all that was required was just so not my forte. I cast about for a solution and voila! I thought of my dear friend and colleague Dianne. She, unlike me, had retired, had the patience, intelligence, and fortitude and most importantly had the time to begin what was for me the incomprehensible process of billing.

DIANNE'S STORY

I was innocently sitting in front of my computer when my dear friend Dr. Julie called with a proposition. Would I be interested in helping her with insurance billing? Naively I thought, hmm, how hard could that be? Of course I would be happy to help.

Oh boy, was I wrong. I had to put on my big girl panties and dive into the rabbit hole. To quote the Grateful Dead, "What a long, strange trip it's been".

I soon realized that this task required far more than just filling out and sending in claims. Unbelievably I actually liked it, which made Dr. Julie question my sanity. She can't find the DSM code for my case but I think she doesn't want me cured.

Slowly but surely I learned some of the ins and outs of the system. This has not been an easy process but eventually the money did start trickling in. I am still learning.

One day Dr. Julie and I were talking about how difficult it must be for the sole practitioner who can't afford to pay someone to tackle the insanity.

We decided to share our experiences with you.

INTRODUCTION

Most likely, if you purchased this book, you have to handle the billing yourself.

That means you are going it alone. We want to help. Our experiences have left us both feeling cracked, crazed and needing therapy as we learned the ropes. (We had purchased the rope for a different reason but this story has a happy ending.)

If you have only a few clients, start now because you have time on your hands in which to learn the ins and outs.

We will share our adventures about what to expect and tips for how you can reduce the frustration and craziness for yourself, ultimately minimizing your need for therapy. We say reduce your frustration and craziness somewhat, because unfortunately there is no way to eliminate it completely--unless of course you are heavily medicated.

Now having scared you silly, why, why, why would you want to go toe to toe with insurance companies? Good Question. Well here's the upside of plunging into the abyss:

1. *The insurance companies send you referrals.*
2. *You don't have to waste your precious funds on advertising.*
3. *You don't have to attend those stultifying networking gatherings.*
4. *If everything is done correctly -- THEY WILL SEND YOU MONEY!*

Our sincere hope is that eventually you can afford to pay someone to do this-- and believe me you will want to pay someone to take on this task as soon as you can. As your clientele increases, it will take more time to deal with the claims.

You need to be working with your clients not spending time with the baffling ever-changing world of insurance billing. Do what Dr. Julie did at that point, find someone who needs some extra money, has the time and give him or her this book. Then you can sit back and be very, very grateful.

In the meantime -- it is worth it. You will get through. Let's plunge in!

CHAPTER 1 FIRST THINGS FIRST

Tips for the Flustered, Flummoxed and Fearful

DO THIS NOW!

Apply online for a National Provider Identifier (NPI)

Really, you have to do this first if you haven't already!

You may ask, "What is a NPI"? All you really need to know about the NPI is that it is a number assigned to you and that the insurance companies require it for billing. The great news is that the NPI is free and easy to get.

Note: They refer to something called a Taxonomy Code. If you don't know what yours is go to the NPI website listed below.

http://www.wpc-edi.com/reference/

At the website scroll down to Behavioral Health and Social Service Providers for the information you need.

The application is called the National Plan and Provider Enumeration System Application. Good grief! I'm sure this makes sense to someone, somewhere. I wonder if they got paid by the word to come up with that one. I had to look up the word "Enumeration" which by the way means "list or record". WTF. (Excuse the expletive it is only the first of many to come.)

> ❖ **TIP**: When filling out your information online be sure to use the back button on the web page vs. your browser back button …I didn't and had to laboriously fill in the information all over again. And again. And so forth.

So, on to the application. There are only three steps to obtain your NPI. Go to this link and give it a minute. This is the NPI application link.

https://nppes.cms.hhs.gov/NPPES/Welcome.do

Talk about immediate gratification…I filled out the application and within five minutes I received an email with the NPI number for Dr. Julie.

If you prefer to call or email, the contact information is on the website. Just be aware that it will take much longer to receive your NPI.

CHAPTER 2 WHAT IS A PANEL, A NETWORK, A PPO, AN HMO?

AND MOST IMPORTANTLY..WHY DO WE GIVE A DARN?

Tips for the Puzzled, Perplexed, and Panicked

All these terms refer to some aspect of how insurance companies interact with us, the mental health providers or if you prefer behavioral health providers.

An insurance panel/network is a registry of therapists who have a contract with the insurance company. This registry is limited to therapists who have completed the company's credentialing process (See Chapter 3) and have been accepted. If you are on an insurance panel you are an in-network provider.

The trick is to get on the panel/network in the first place. This depends mostly on your credentials, your specialization and how many other therapists there are in your area.

> ❖ **TIP**: If you have a specialty, flaunt it. Make sure to emphasize your training and experience.

There are two types of panels: Preferred Provider Organizations (*PPO*s) and Health Management Organizations (*HMO*s).

It is important to understand that clients who have an *HMO* insurance plan can only work with providers who are in the *HMO* network. For providers to be in-network they must go through the *HMO*'s credentialing process, have been approved and are then considered to be in their network or on their panel. The provider must contact the *HMO* directly and/or go online for an application. Once you have provided them with the required information it usually takes them at least three months to complete the approval.

Having said that some *HMOs* will allow non-network providers to provide services but the client must pay a larger percentage of the cost in addition to a deductible and/or copay.

PPOs work with both in-network and out-of-network providers. What is important for you to know is that *PPOs* are insurance companies that are set up so that the client can select their own treatment providers. The *PPO* will have a list of preferred providers who are in their network but the client is free to go outside that group for treatment. With out–of-network providers there may be a larger deductible that has to be met before the company pays. And then the client may have a larger copay or not, depending on their insurance plan. (We warned you didn't we?)

With a *PPO* you will have to find out what the patient's copay is and what your reimbursement will be. Sometimes they pay 100% of your charge, sometimes it is a percentage of your charge, *usual and customary*, with the patient picking up the balance. Other times, who knows what the pluck they will pay. You have to ask.

One would assume that an in-network provider would be paid at a higher rate than an out-of-network provider....one would be SO wrong. In-network providers agree to payment for services at a lower rate. The upside is, once in-network, the insurance company will send you referrals. So you have to decide which is more important: to have more clients at a reduced rate, fewer clients or none at all.

CHAPTER 3 CREDENTIALING

Tips for the Curious, Crabby and Clueless

Credentialing is the process whereby the insurance company verifies your credentials -- go figure. This is a big deal and entails a lot of paperwork. Insurance companies may not be enthusiastic about your application because it costs them money to credential you and maintain your information.

Some insurance companies require a prescreening application before they even send you an official application. This can usually be found on the insurance company website. You need to determine whether you are filing for a prescreening or an actual application.

After you have filled out the actual credentialing application make sure to find out what the time limit is for them to receive all your information. This is important because if some information is missing or incomplete, they won't necessarily let you know. When the time limit has passed and your information is incomplete you are then "timed out" (their terminology). If you are "timed out" you have to start all over again. Poor baby.

> ❖ **TIP**: To avoid this eventuality you will have to stay on top of them. (No we didn't mean THAT! Just making sure you're awake.) So it is worth the time to mark your calendar to periodically call and check on your application

For those of you who have actually entered the 21st century, the following tip is for you.

> ❖ **TIP**: Get your smart phone out and set an alarm to follow up and ensure they received the initial packet. I suggest you call every few weeks and ask if there are any problems.

If you are rejected (Boo Hoo) there are a couple of other strategies.

- *If you have a specialty, you can contact the insurance company and ask how many other specialists are providing those services in your area.*

- *Call and verify the number of other in-network providers in your town. The people at the insurance company may be counting providers in your entire county. If you, however, provide services in one small area of that county they need to know this and may accept your application*

In closing, Dr. J encourages you to get on panels because as mentioned before

THEY SEND YOU REFERRALS!

CAQH
Council for Affordable Quality Healthcare

You may see or hear about something called CAQH. Not to worry. Here is what you need to know.

CAQH hosts a universal credentialing database for healthcare providers.

When a provider requests participation in a network that accepts the CAQH application, the insurance company initiates an online account for the provider. The provider then completes the online application submitting several supporting documents to CAQH.

Once you are in the CAQH database then any insurance company that accepts the CAQH application can access the provider's information, expediting the credentialing process. The number of insurance companies that accept the CAQH application is increasing all the time.

Once you are accepted by CAQH you will still be required to sign a contract with the insurance company. CAQH reduces the application process but it is not a contract.

Medicare

Medicare is a federal program providing health insurance coverage to people 65 and over, those with permanent genetic disabilities, and those who meet other criteria.

In order to submit Medicare claims you will have to be registered directly with Medicare. Individual insurance companies don't register you to be a Medicare provider.

Only certain types of licensures are acceptable to Medicare. You can go to their website to determine whether you are eligible to even apply. Your professional organization may have that information also.

It is also important to recognize that Medicare is a national program. Your license has been awarded to you by the state in which you live. Therefore it is possible that you will be required to also have a national certification, which usually requires that you take a certifying test to qualify as a Medicare provider. Are we having fun yet?

CHAPTER 4 THE CRYPTIC AND CHALLENGING CMS 1500

Tips for the Confused, Constipated and Chaotic

I have used some very colorful terminology when referring to the CMS 1500 but in our tome, decided to go with cryptic and challenging, a more mature approach. I first want to prepare you for the overwhelming confusion you may experience the first few times you work with this form. It is normal. Do not be discouraged. Even today when I have to fill out one of these forms my eyes cross, glaze over and bad words pop out of my mouth.

Then they went and changed the form just as I got comfortable with the present form. Most of the form remains the same so I will indicate a few of the changes as [NF:] I strongly suggest you go to the NUCC.org website for further details.

WHAT THE &#!# GOES WHERE?

Take it just one block at a time and you don't have to understand or know why.

If I can do this--you can do this.

When you complete this form for each client we suggest reading the explanations below and as you fill in each block check it off and move on to the next block as directed. It becomes easier each time. Get out your magnifying glass and refer to the sample CMS 1500 form and observe each block carefully.

_____Block 1. If you don't know for sure…select "other".

_____Block 1a. INSURED'S ID NUMBER. As you look at the client's insurance card, there may be several numbers; the one you are looking for is the ID number (not group or plan number). I know what you are thinking, how hard can that be; but on one card the ID number is in really small print while the group number is in large letters…are they trying to make it hard for us? Enter the insured person's Insurance ID number from their insurance card. Check it twice.

> ❖ TIP: MAKE A COPY OF THE INSURANCE CARD FRONT AND BACK TO HAVE ON FILE. Make sure you can read the copy. If the client's name on the CMS 1500 is not spelled exactly as it is written on the card or if the number is wrong you have just wasted a lot of time.

_____Block 2. PATIENT'S NAME and Block 4.INSURED PERSON'S NAME: It seems obvious but what to enter into Boxes 2 and 4 can be confusing. You need to make sure who the insured person is (Block 4) and who the patient is (Block 2). Obviously it can be the same but not necessarily. Block 2 is where patient information goes. That might be the insured person, the spouse, the child or other. Block 4 is where insured person's name/ information goes. Note if 2 and 4 are the same person there is no need to fill in address, etc. in Block 7.

____Block 3. BIRTHDATE: You absolutely HAVE TO HAVE THE INSURED PERSON'S DATE OF BIRTH! ! Insurance companies demand you provide the birthdate before they will process any claim. Also you MUST indicate M (male) or F (female). They will not process the claim without sex. (That got you going didn't it? Gotta have some fun here.)

____Block 4. INSURED PERSON'S NAME: You MUST enter the name EXACTLY as it is on the insurance card. Don't you hate it when they tell you what you MUST do?

____Block 5. PATIENT'S ADDRESS: You really don't need directions here do you?

____Block 6. PATIENT RELATIONSHIP TO INSURED: Check relationship to insured. It is not always self.

____Block 7. INSURED PERSON'S ADDRESS: When the insured person, patient and address are the same, you can write the word "same" in this block.

____Block 8. PATIENT STATUS: Self explanatory [NF: This is blank].

____Block 9 a-d. OTHER INSURED'S NAME: If Block 11d (Is there another health plan) is marked YES.... then Block 9 a-d must be completed. [NF: 9b-c is now blank].

____Block 10. IS PATIENT'S CONDITION RELATED TO: You can figure this one out but if the answer is NO then you still must enter NO.

____Block 10d. RESERVED FOR LOCAL USE: Leave it blank. New Form: I have no idea what this is about. Check the website.

____Block 11. INSURED'S POLICY GROUP OR FECA NUMBER: This information is optional -- sometimes this information is on the insurance card and sometimes it isn't. This information is not required to process the claim.

____Block 11a. INSURED'S DATE OF BIRTH: Fill in only if Block 2 and 4 are different.

____Block 11b-c. If information is on the card fill this in but it may not be so don't worry about it.

____Block 11d. IS THERE ANOTHER HEALTH BENEFIT PLAN?: Notice the very small print that directs you back to blocks 9 a-d.

____Block 12. PATIENT'S/AUTHORIZED PERSON'S SIGNATURE: Have your client sign and date a CMS 1500 and keep it in their file. For all future claims you can write "Signature on file" in this block.

____Block 13. INSURED/AUTHORIZED PERSON'S SIGNATURE: In addition to Block 12 have your client sign and date Bock 13. This authorizes the insurance company to pay you directly. When completing the form write in "SOF" (signature on file) otherwise they will pay the client directly. And you know what happens then.

> ❖ TIP: Even though insurance companies have the demographic data on the client, according to HIPPA, sending in a claim equals our sending private information about the client to an outside source. Hence, you better be sure to have them sign Blocks 12 and 13 and keep it on file.

____Blocks 14-20. We don't normally deal with these but if you do, call the insurance company for further information.

____Block 21 1-4. See the numbers 1. _____ 2. _____ 3. _____ 4. _____

The DSM diagnosis codes are entered in these blocks. You can enter up to 4 diagnoses in order: primary, secondary, etc. You must have at least one.

> ❖ TIP: Diagnosis codes: I have found that one can -- Google codes. If you don't want to scan through that huge DSM-V.... just Google it. The world according to Google is amazing.

NOTE For the future, or possibly yesterday, depending on when you are reading this book, we also have to talk about ICD-11-CM codes. These are not the same as DSM codes but will some day, at least in the insurance world, replace them. These are now found in the DSM 5 for our convenience. When they will be required is anyone's guess.

For now in the upper right corner of block 21 you will see ICD ind. In the space following put the number 9. We are still using ICD9. Experts believe we will never use ICD 10 but will skip right to ICD 11.

> ❖ TIP: Check it out: Some insurance companies do not accept V codes. Some insurance companies don't pay for sexual disorder diagnoses. And then there are those that only accept V Codes. Confused? Join the club. You need to call and ask.

____Block 22. MEDICAID RESUBMISSION: Our experience does not cover Medicaid or Medicare issues. So, unfortunately, with this block you are on your own.

____Block 23. PRIOR AUTHORIZATION NUMBER: If the insurance company requires preauthorization for services and they give you an authorization number - - this is where that number goes. If preauthorization is required and you don't write in the number they will deny the claim. Yes even though they have that number in their records we have to give it to them again. Think they are messing with us? Some insurance companies don't bother with a number….you have to find out which companies do and which don't.

Blocks 24 A-J. Has lots of stuff to fill in. This same form is used for medical as well as behavioral claims so it might get confusing. I'll explain. Let's get started.

I am sure you know this but some of us go into trance when we see this kind of paperwork so…. for each visit you will need to fill in the information from 24 A. to 24 J. working across the page. Look at the form, it will make more sense.

____Block 24 A. DATES OF SERVICE: If the month or day of the month is a single digit put a zero in front of it. Example January 1 would be 01/01. Now here is another place to be careful. Do they want 2013 or just 13 or whatever the year is? Look carefully at the form. You must write the date twice across, once under the "From" column and again under the "To" column.

____Block 24 B. PLACE OF SERVICE: Requires a number that indicates where the service was performed. For a therapist it is usually at the office. That would be the number 11. Just write in "11" in block 24B

____Block 24 C. Ignore this.

____Block 24 D. CPT/HCPCS CODES AND MODIFIER: Don't worry about HCPCS codes -- these refer to medical procedures. I have not had to enter a Modifier as yet in a claim. We do have to enter a CPT code. CPT codes have to do with the type of appointment and length of visit.

> ❖ TIP: To find the latest CPT codes go to www.ama-assn.org/go/cpt.

____Block 24 E. DIAGNOSIS POINTER: Just put the number "1" in this block. If you want to know why read on. Look back at Block 21. Most of us will only have one diagnosis, which will be written in Block 21.1. So in Block 24 you enter the number "1" which refers back to 21.1 where the diagnosis is already entered. Don't ask….I have no idea and I really don't want to know. It must make sense somewhere in their universe.

____Block 24 F. CHARGES: Finally after all your hard work your fee goes here. No matter what they say they will pay do not under any circumstances play the "What do I think they will actually pay" game or even try to compute this in any way. I have learned to always enter the full fee here. The insurance companies will compute the payment amounts and believe me it is usually less than your full fee.

____Block 24 G. DAYS OR UNITS: Enter the number "1" in this block. The number "1" means one visit that corresponds to the date in Block 24A

____Block 24 H. EPSDT: Refers to a Medicaid program that provides services for children. We are not addressing Medicaid in this text.

____Block 24 I. ID QUAL In the block next to NPI put your NPI number here.

____Block 24 J. RENDERING PROVIDER ID: Write your NPI number here

____Block 25. FEDERAL TAX ID NUMBER: Enter your EIN number if you have a business or your Social Security Number. Make sure to put an "X" in either SSN or EIN.

____Block 26. PATIENT'S ACCOUNT NO: This is left blank unless you choose to assign your patient an ID number. If you choose to do this, put your number for that patient here and it will be added to the payment summary that the insurance company returns to you…. hopefully with some money attached. Don't confuse this with the number in Block 1A. That is the number the insurance company has given the client. Block 26 is a number you assign to your client for your own records.

____Block 27. ACCEPT ASSIGNMENT?: IMPORTANT! MUST BE CHECKED "YES". This block checked with a YES along with "SOF" in block 13 authorizes the insurance company to pay you directly. Remember, if this is not checked YES, the money will not come to you.

____Block 28. TOTAL CHARGE: Total charges for all visits on this claim -- get that adding machine out. We are counselors not accountants.

____Block 29. AMOUNT PAID: The copay amount would go here but I never fill that in. It's up to you on this one.

____Block 30. BALANCE DUE: This should be the same amount as Block 28.

____Block 31. SIGNATURE: You sign with your credentials and date here.

____Block 32. SERVICE FACILITY LOCATION INFORMATION: The address of the office where services are provided.

____Block 33. BILLING PROVIDER INFO & PH#: Address where you receive your mail for your business. These can be the same or not as your office or not but fill it in. Don't forget your telephone number.

____Block 33a. NPI goes here again… NO, we don't care why, we just want to make sure we are reimbursed for our services. So just do it.

> ❖ TIP: Beginning in 2014 a new CMS 1500 will be in use. Please check the website for details. www.nucc.org. Basically the same form with minimal changes.

Submitting Claims

There are three ways I know of to submit claims.

1. Fill out CMS 1500 form by hand and mail it to the address supplied by the insurance company. Be sure to ask for the behavioral health billing mailing address. There are also software programs that you can buy that allow you to fill in the form on the computer, print it out and mail it in. We chose not to spend the money because all but one of the claims we send in can be done online.

2. Use the website of the insurance company to send in claims. You will have to register online with the website and directions will take you through the process.

3. Use a clearinghouse. A clearinghouse is an organization that provides service for specific insurance companies. You use this service to submit the claim online with the clearinghouse. They make sure all the necessary information has been entered correctly and then will send it on to the insurance company. This process just makes sure the information is entered into the right blocks but does not verify the accuracy of the information.

The insurance company will direct you to clearinghouses that you can use to submit their claim. For example when I have a Cigna or Blue Cross client I use Office Ally. You will have to register with the clearinghouse.

To register with the clearinghouse, all you have to do is fill out the required information and they will send you a link and temporary password. Then it is a matter of learning the ins and outs of that particular website. They will have training available. It is pretty simple but there is a learning curve.

Office Ally was my first clearinghouse experience. It was unforgettable. I've been faithful ever since. They have technical support personnel who actually answer the phone and even better, don't make you feel stupid.

Even if using online claim submission you will need to know what goes in the different blocks on the CMS 1500 because they require the same information.

> ❖ TIP: ALWAYS make a copy of the claim you are submitting. I repeat always make a copy of the claim. Often there is a link that says PRINT. Other times I just do a print screen....if there's a glitch, you have proof!

CHAPTER 5 CALLING INSURANCE COMPANIES

Tips for the Intimidated, Innocent, Inexperienced

Here are some reasons you might contact an insurance company:

- *Call to find out what coverage your client has.*

- *Some policies will require pre-authorization, some don't.*

- *Some have limited number of visits after which you need to submit a preauthorization request.*

- *Some don't need preauthorization but have limited visits per year.*

- *Some have time limits within which sessions must be concluded.*

- *Some pay in full, some clients pay a copay. Are we having fun yet????*

OK, so just make a call. Sounds easy, right? It can be easy but it can also feel like Alice falling down the rabbit hole.

So

   follow

      us

         down…

Here are a couple of our experiences in Insuranceland.

> *After I checked the client's insurance card I went to the Abba Dabba website listed on the back. The Abba Dabba Insurance Company website referred me to Company Boop Poop a Doop who handled all their behavioral heath claims. Understand right now that most insurance companies have other insurance companies (or I don't know what they call the other organizations) to handle their behavioral health claim.*
>
> *I went online and trudged through the process to be able to access their website to submit claims--only to find out Abba Dabba had been purchased by Company Caca, which within a very short time was gobbled up by Company Dooda. I now am working very nicely with Company DooDa but who knows how long before the Queen of Hearts goes after this one too.*

Be prepared for this shell game. It is the reality of dealing with THEM. You will be better off if you just relax, accept, and keep on checking.

> *On another occasion, a new client had Honky Donky Insurance so I innocently submitted the claim to Honky Donky Insurance Company only to have it returned - rejected and unpaid. This is mystifying because Dr. J is an in-network provider with this company and I had processed many claims for other clients with Honky Donky Insurance Company. Why would this time be any different?*
>
> *Well, It was time to make a CALL. Now remember, Honky Donky Insurance does handle mental health claims but it just so happens that this particular client had a different kind of policy and they farmed out the mental health claims to another company. I had to resubmit the claim to Company Xanadu…this required another call, extra time and added to the workload because I already did this once and here I go again. In the meantime we are not paid and WE ARE NOT HAPPY…*

AND NOW TO WORK

When dealing with insurance companies' seemingly Machiavellian practices, paranoia can easily creep in. You can begin to see them as evil and out to get you. This can be true but it won't get you paid. And over time this attitude can deteriorate into a 5150 and screaming into the telephone. Let's not go there.

In the beginning, I went in with the attitude that the claims department was going to be perverse, persnickety, and a pain in the patootie,. With that outlook I was never disappointed -- they met my every expectation. Over time I became gaunt and bitter.

For my own benefit I had to let go of that mindset. I now approach this whole calling insurance companies from a stance of needing and asking for their help versus seeing them as the enemy. I do much better when I mentally prepare myself in this way.

> - TIP: First thing to do when you call is to ASK FOR HELP.
> - Remember to sound needy.
> - I will remind you of this because it is critical to your peace of mind and increases the chance you will get helped.

After you get your Zen on, asking for help begins the process with a whole different energy. Getting snippy gets zilch done, it takes longer to get zilch done and most people on the other end of the line truly do want to be helpful.

Remember they only work there they don't set policy.

THE FIRST CALL IS THE HARDEST

<u>Have the following information on hand before you make any call:</u>

☐ 1. Copy of insurance card if possible

☐ 2. Your NPI#_____ and your Tax ID#_____

☐ 3. Patient name as shown on insurance card

☐ 4. Insured person's insurance ID number from card. For military use the SSN

☐ 5. Patient's Date Of Birth

☐ 6. Insured Person's name (if different)

☐ 7. Insured person's DOB Don't even bother to call if you don't have the DOB.

<u>Where to call</u>:

Look at the tiny print on the back of the card for the phone number. Determine whether there is a separate phone number for Mental Health. You might find not only a different phone number but you might even find a different insurance company listed for mental health/behavioral health services. Make sure to look.

For example if your client has Honky Donky Insurance you may have to bill Abba Dabba for mental health services. This is called a "carve-out". Why is it called that you ask….hell if I know and I don't really care.

If there is no separate phone number, when you reach a real person (good luck with that) ask if this is the right number for mental health/behavioral health queries.

❖ TIP: When calling insurance companies make sure you DOCUMENT, DOCUMENT, and oh don't forget to DOCUMENT!

Make note of the phone number you called.

Note the name of the customer representative you spoke with.

Write dates, times, and what was said. Especially make note of what they are going to do and when. Put the note in the patient's chart.

AND get a reference number for your call before you hang up so that when you call back they can look up the record of your conversation.

> *I just had a call (no really, I did) from a precertification department denying a request for services. They referred me to another department called Provider Inquiries for specific information on why it was denied and what could be done. I verified that I had written down the right phone number and the title of the department I was calling. Just before we disconnected I remembered to ask if there was a reference number to use in the next call….there was. I don't know why they rarely offer that reference number unless asked. I verified that when I called the Provider Inquiry department I would use that number. Whew. I almost forgot to follow my own suggestion. When I got to the next person that number saved time and sanity.*

❖ TIP: Remember to breathe deeply, relax and be prepared to be on the phone for a while. I guarantee if you get the answers to your questions in your first contact you are saving yourself time, sweat, tears and most important saving $$.

Reasons to Call and What to Ask

New Client

First call. Here we go. Ask for the following information when you call:

1. Is this the right department for behavioral health claims? Always ask this. I can't tell you how many times I went through my whole spiel only to find out I was talking to the medical side of the house. Yes they separate medical from behavioral.

2. Once you have the right department -- get ready for the Academy Awards -- always begin with: "Can you help me?" (Remember to sound really needy!!!).

3. Is the client eligible for mental health services? It is a good practice to do this before you see the client. Sometimes they have to obtain authorization prior to services rendered.

4. Verify the name of the company that handles mental health services.

Questions to ask about Benefits:

1. Is precertification/ preauthorization required?

  . If so: where can you obtain copy of the form? Online? Can it be faxed?

*2. Where do you send the precertification form?
If you can fax it in, verify the correct behavioral health fax number. You can't rely on the accuracy of the fax number on the form. This is important because some clients may have Honky Donky Insurance but guess what, you may have to submit the preauthorization form to a different fax number.*

3. Do the mental health benefits cover parity and non-parity diagnoses? Get as much detail as you can on non-parity coverage.

4. Is there a deductible? If so how much?

5. Does client pay a copay? If so, how much?

6. If not a copay then does client pay coinsurance? If so, how much?

7. Is the number of visits limited?

    a. Is the limit per year, per week, etc?

    b. If limited how do you request more services?

8. What company processes the claims? Sounds like a stupid question but remember these may not be same company.

9. Can I submit the claim online with the company?

    a. If so, obtain the website information. You will have to register on the website before you can utilize the online services.

    b. If not, which clearinghouses do they use?

10. If the claim needs to be mailed, ask for the mailing address for behavioral health claims -- don't rely on the insurance card for this. Mailing is rare these days.

11. Ask for the contact phone number where you can inquire about claims after they have been submitted. Just our luck, the number to verify claims can be different than the one to verify eligibility. And sometimes the number for verification of eligibility is different than the one to determine what the coverage is. Eligibility just means they are covered by that insurance. Benefits or coverage is actually what the company will pay for.

<u>Client requires more sessions</u>

Call to request for preauthorization/precertification for more sessions: (Just a reminder that preauthorization and precertification means the same darn thing.)

    1. First you have to ask for the most recent precertification form.

    2. Also, the form itself may stay the same but may have a different company name or a different fax number. (Remember Abba Dabba and Honky Donky?). Always best to be sure each time.

    3. They will either fax you a form or tell you where to find it online. Some forms you can fill in online and print out and fax. Others you can print out but

have to fill in by hand. If that is the case, fill it in, scan and fax it.

> ❖ TIP: You can NEVER EVER use standard email to send client information as per HIPPA regulations.

An important note on precertification or preauthorization…once you have one there are some issues to be aware of.

- ➢ The number of sessions is limited. Keep track as you complete sessions

- ➢ There is usually a specific time frame within which the sessions must be completed. That means that if you don't get the approved sessions accomplished within the dates listed you must apply for another preauthorization.

- ➢ Check to see how they date the beginning of the authorization. Some will begin the new sessions beginning on the day in which they receive your application. If you have not finished all sessions on previous preauthorization you lose them. Yup…they are gone. So you don't want to fax in preauthorization until the day you finish the sessions.

- ➢ Some companies will let you determine the beginning date of sessions. You just have to read over the form to find out. AND I would suggest you call and verify.

Here is a cautionary tale

> *Once upon a time Dianne followed the procedure to request additional sessions. She got the paperwork showing 20 visits had been approved…yea. Something made her check the date range of the approved time frame. Lo and behold, they had given a whole 14 weeks in which to complete 20 sessions. Hmmm. Now you and I both know that they are not going to pay for more than one session per week. She had to call them back and very nicely ask them to extend the time frame. They did.*

> ❖ **TIP:** Make a note on your calendar when the number of sessions is close to being completed or the time limit is near. Call to find out what to do to receive approval for more visits. Do this in a timely manner. Ask how long the approval process takes. You don't want to wait for them to mail you the paperwork. It takes forever.

> ❖ Ask for the phone number to call after the paperwork is submitted to verify approval. Make sure you ask for the right number to call. Yes, yes, yet another number. You can never go wrong asking for the specific phone number. Sigh!

A continuation of the above story…..I called about a claim but got the precertification department. On a hunch since I was there I decided to verify the date change, which supposedly had been done when I called the last time. Lo and behold…. they had not noted the date change. They still had the original ending date. The nice person on the phone said she would make that change right away. This time I asked her to fax me the paperwork. If you have that in hand there is nothing they can do.

> ❖ TIP: Make sure you have it in writing.

Call yearly to verify that the client still has coverage.

Call to verify benefits--annually or biannually. I am so sorry to have to tell you this but sometimes the insurance coverage changes, or the client no longer has insurance with that company. Policies can change at any time.

Calling in a panic because the claim was denied

We have a whole chapter on this subject. If this is your concern go immediately to Chapter 6.

Calling because they paid you WHAT?

You received the explanation of benefits (EOB) and yea you got paid….BUT the amount paid wasn't quite what you expected. You call because you want clarification and their justification of how they came up with that paltry amount.

- BEWARE. BE PREPARED. Know if you are in- or out-of-network with this company and what the client's benefits are before you call.
- Believe it or not sometimes they make a mistake and will correct it.
- Know what your contract says if you have one.

- Know what your contracted rate for this client is. That is in your contract.

I have called and asked about amounts paid and the answers I received were gobble-de-goop. They talk really fast and say stuff that makes absolutely no sense. But they say it with such conviction it is hard to ask for an explanation. When you do ask their explanation is as confusing as what was originally stated.

Barbara C. Griswold, LMFT has given us an explanation of what she calls "Insurance Speak".

We are so grateful to her for this clearly stated explanation. She has done those of us doing our own insurance a great service.

To understand the examples in the table on the next page, you need to know that the provider's contracted rate with the insurance company is $67. You have to know that in order to make sense of what they tell you when you call, so read on and learn some amazing, crazy stuff. Hang on to your hats and if you are like me, mathematically challenged, you will have to read this more than once.

What the Representative Tells You	What Jack Will Have To Pay	What Insurance Will Pay
"He has a $10 copayment, after which he is covered at 100 percent of the contracted rate," or "he is covered at 100 percent with a $10 copayment."	Ignore the "100 percent" part of the sentence. Jack will pay $10 (his copayment) per session.	$57. To calculate, take your contracted rate of $67, and subtract Jack's copayment of $10
"Jack is covered at 70 percent."	Since the plan is paying 70%, Jack must pay 30 percent of your contracted rate of $67, a total of **$20.10** per session.	$46.90 (70 percent of the contracted rate of $67)
"Jack is covered at 90 percent, up to a maximum of $25 per session."	Don't waste your time figuring out what 90 percent of your contracted rate is. The rep is telling you that the most CureQuick will pay per session is $25. Jack pays the difference between the $25 insurance reimbursement and the contracted rate of $67, which is **$42**.	$25
"Jack has a deductible of $150, and none of it has been used. After that he is covered at 90 percent.	Here things get interesting. All of Sessions 1 and 2 will go toward the deductible, so Jack will pay $67 for each session, using up $134 of the deductible. In Session 3, Jack must pay $16 of your $67 fee to finish the deductible, plus 10 percent of the remaining $51 ($16 + $5.10 = $21.10). After this he will pay 10 percent of your contracted rate, or $6.70 per session.	For Session 1 and 2, insurance pays $0. For Session 3, the plan pays $45.90 ($67 minus Jack's copay of $21.10). After this, the plan pays 90 percent of $67, or $60.30 per session.

"Reprinted with permission from **Navigating the Insurance Maze: The Therapist's Complete Guide to Working With Insurance – And Whether You Should** (Fifth Edition, pg 42), by Barbara Griswold, LMFT; Paper Street Press, 2014: San Jose, CA"

www.theinsurancemaze.com

40

CHAPTER 6 CLAIM DENIED! DON'T PANIC!!

Tips for the Disillusioned, Dismayed and Discouraged

Unless you have a Histrionic Personality Disorder, you don't need to panic. Know that claims are ALWAYS being denied somewhere in the insurance universe. It may seem deliberate but let's not go there unless you also have a Paranoid Personality Disorder or Paranoid Histrionic Personality Disorder. For the rest of us let's begin with:

Why, why, why are claims denied?

- Insurance companies make mistakes; it's not always our error.

    Solution: NEVER just accept a denial…call immediately and ask WTF… but do it with a really good attitude.

- Client's name is inaccurate or misspelled

    Solution: Make a clear copy of the card and use the name as it is spelled on the card. Names must be identical.

- Birth date is incorrect.

    Solution: Question client closely about why they are lying about their age. Get the right birthdate.

- Insurance identification number is inaccurate.

    Solution: Fill this in when you are sober. Again, get a clear copy of the card or if client giving the number verbally verify.

- Information on the CMS 1500 is missing. You have seen this demented form. It is so easy to forget something, it happens to us all.

    Solution: Remember our checklist in Chapter 4.

- Client has not met their deductible for the year.

    Solution: This is the reason you must call at the beginning of services to check the client's insurance coverage. You will have to submit the claims anyway and will not get paid by the insurance company until deductible is met. Client pays until insurance kicks in.

- Insurance coverage has changed in the middle of the year.

    Solution: One of those things in life you can't control.

- Client has changed insurance companies and "forgot" to mention it.

    Solution: According to Dr. Julie we call this unresolved hostility. Get copy of new insurance card and call them to determine benefits.

- They deny claim for your initial assessment.

    Solution: FYI, Insurance companies will only pay for one assessment per year. If your client has seen another therapist who submitted that charge you are out of luck.

- You needed an authorization and didn't get it.

    Solution: When making the initial call to insurance company regarding eligibility and benefits always ask whether precertification is required.

- You have an authorization but you have exceeded the number of authorized visits or time allotted to complete sessions.

    Solution: That means if your authorization is for 12 sessions from September 1 to December 1 of same year and you forget to request more sessions you will not be paid; so you need authorization after 12 sessions or if the 12 sessions go beyond the December 1 deadline. No, I am not making this up. Yes, you are left high and dry and unpaid. Although some companies will have you send in clinical notes for sessions not covered and they might pay a portion of your contracted fee. CALL.

WHAT CAN YOU DO WHEN A CLAIM IS DENIED

You will have the scary experience of having a claim denied. OK the first few times you will panic, you will get exceedingly irritated, probably say several really bad words, then after counting to 10, meditating or medicating, whichever works for you, take a few deep breaths and calmly call the insurance company

> ❖ TIP: Usually it is a simple fix and all you have to do is resubmit whatever you forgot -- see if you can fax it for quickest results. Ask what the subject line should be and to whom should it be addressed. Be sure to verify the fax number. Even if you have it -- VERIFY. They change numbers. Also ask for a reference number for this call.

When you call remember to BREATHE deeply and relax. Tell the person who answers that you hope they can help you do what you need to do to get this claim accepted and paid. They have to tell you.

It might just be some information that was not provided by you on the CMS 1500. It might be because the number of authorized visits has lapsed. It might be that the client has gotten married and the name has changed. Or maybe it was denied because it was raining. Or somebody has gas. There are a million reasons. You just have to ask and keep asking for help to correct this claim.

Have the following checklist on hand before you pick up the phone.

☐ Client's name as printed on card

☐ Client's insurance ID number from the card or SSN.

☐ Birth date (This is absolutely mandatory in any conversation with insurance companies about a client.)

☐ Your tax ID number or NPI number.

☐ Date of service (DOS) about which you are calling. DOS is always vital.

☐ A notepad. Keep a record of the phone number(s) you called and what they said.

The person on the insurance end of the phone line is usually a very nice person. They don't always have the answers or even the right answers but I encourage you to ASK for their help. Be prepared to be transferred -- endlessly.

PERSISTENCE is the key. The answers are somewhere in the system. Keep asking. Several phone calls later you will most likely have an answer. Might not always like the answer but they have to give you one.

> ❖ TIP: Don't just accept the denial....call and ask WTF....but remember to ask the question with a really *good* attitude.

Very Important Story of Lesson Learned

- **Beware**... *when Dr. J was young and naïve about the denizens of the Insuranceworld, an Abba Dabba representative with a very friendly, very soothing voice called and induced her to reduce the amount she was being paid from 100% to 75% of her fee. You might wonder why she would agree to that...well, the very gently persuasive representative, gave the impression that Dr. J would be wise to agree to the reduction if she wanted to remain a provider with this company... this among other reasons, is why Dr. J needs me.*

An insurance billing expert at a conference assured us that Dr. J did not have to accept the lower rate. Apparently this is a common practice by insurance companies to have a very friendly, very engaging person call you and deceitfully try to get you to accept a reduction in payment.

> ❖ **TIP**: Do not accept or agree to any reduction in payment. You don't have to and they can't make you. So there!

More to this story:

- *As if that weren't bad enough, a few months later I received a fax from another company representing Abba Dabba. It was significant because in this fax they had the gall to state that if we signed the form immediately and faxed it back, Dr. J. would receive a whopping $30 per session. No we did not say an additional $30 but a total of $30 per session. Wow - according to them we really needed to jump on that to get paid right away! Sneaky weasels. (Our apologies to weasels everywhere.)*

CHAPTER 7 KEEPING TRACK OF CLIENTS AND COMPANIES

Tips for the Canny, Cunning and Calculating

Beginning with your first phone call to an insurance company, write down the initial phone number, name of insurance company and all other numbers you may be referred to or have to call. When finished with the call transfer this information to a list that you keep of all insurance companies with which you have clients. This is one of those things you just have to experience yourself in order to understand the why.

Make your own listing of the insurance companies. On the list have the mental health department phone number. As already mentioned, many companies have a totally different phone number for mental health services. Also list the insurance company website.

I have a list of all insurance company phone numbers, my user names and passwords for the websites.

I also have the information (phone number for customer service, website, password) for the clearinghouses along with the insurance companies.

> ❖ TIP: This will save you time when you have to call the company again. As time goes on you will have multiple numbers for multiple companies and it gets confusing to keep it all straight

There are many forms out there for you to have client sign to comply with HIPPA. For insurance purposes you will need a release of information on file. Easiest is to use the CMS 1500. You will find Signature Block #12, which covers the release of information for the insurance company. Y*early* have the client sign and date and keep on file. Yes you need a new signature every year.

When you have the client sign their CMS 1500 every year that is a good time to ask if insurance has changed in any way. We had one client who forgot to let us know for months.

When Dr. Julie gives me the list of clients she has seen for the week, I first enter the information on the Excel data worksheet I have set up. There is software out there and it is expensive. If you can afford it great, we couldn't so I developed an Excel Worksheet that has worked for me as the billing manager. I don't have to use the client's clinical file. I only use the demographic information.

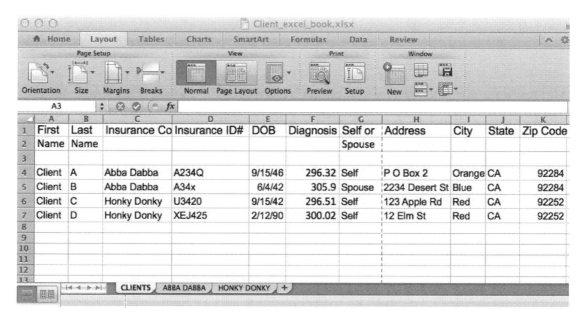

I find it helpful to have this file available on hand in order to submit insurance claims without having to pull out the client's chart every time. I keep separate insurance files for each client.

> ❖ TIP: And as a matter of fact the financial information is not supposed to be kept with the clinical record.

When you call you will be asked for this information and depending on the company they will not answer any questions unless you have this information available. Date of Birth is ALWAYS required even if you have the insurance ID number, address, name, astrological sign, etc. No DOB no deal.

So to summarize: Name, Date of Birth and Insurance ID# is minimum required when you make a call to find out anything on any client.

Here is a sample of how I keep track of client visits. Client A requires a preauthorization. I enter the dates and number of approved visits (20) under client's name. and to keep track I number each visit. Client B has no limit on number of visits so I don't have to number sessions.

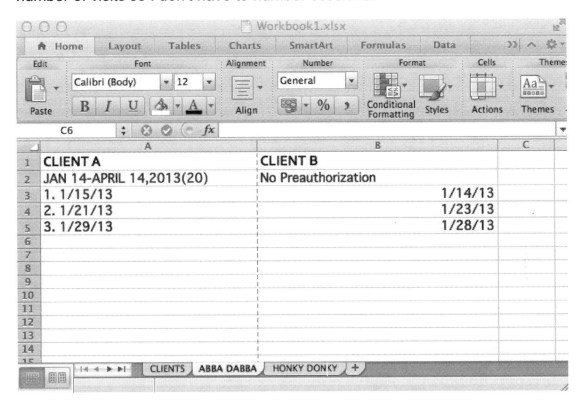

As you can see at the bottom of this graphic there is a separate tab for each insurance company. This is the client list for Abba Dabba Insurance. The Excel program allows for multiple tabs with different information on each.

CHAPTER 8 EAP EMPLOYEE ASSISTANCE PROGRAM

Tips for the Exhilarated, Elastic, and Ecstatic

So far we've been focused on the evils of insurance companies. But guess what? Just yesterday as Dianne and I were bemoaning the hoops that we had to jump through and the number of medications we had to take, I got a call from ABBA DABBA insurance company.

They said, " We have an EAP client for you". I said, "Fabulous".

The evil insurance company had actually invited me into a whole new realm of income. Although they had me fill out a myriad of forms, it turns out I only needed to actually send in my invoice. Knowing how tricky, cunning and baffling these companies are I have kept all the forms they say they don't need.

How It Works

During the initial phone call the insurance company provides the name, phone number and authorization number for the client.

Then the client calls to make an appointment. The insurance company is informed that an appointment has been made. Soon after, I receive an official authorization letter and all of the aforementioned forms. Guess what, I never hear from the insurance company again until they send my check. Can you dig it?

The EAP process only allows for a predetermined number of sessions. After completion of those sessions the client can choose to continue treatment with me through the insurance company's regular behavioral health coverage.

So essentially they are paying me to market myself to individual EAP clients. Could it get better than that?

> TIP: Knowing what I know now, I suppose a crafty therapist could call the insurance companies and inquire about their EAP programs. Why wait?

CHAPTER 9 WHAT IS TRICARE AND WHY SHOULD YOU CARE?

Tips for the Tongue-Tied, Tempestuous and Turbulent

TRICARE is the health care program serving Uniformed Service members, retirees, and their families worldwide. This Department of Defense health care program provides health care coverage including behavioral health care.

We decided to include a chapter on TRICARE because it is a good resource for clients and there are some things unique to this overall system of care. Sharing our experiences may help you if you decide to become one of their providers, especially if you live near a military facility.

It is worthwhile working with Tricare but it can be very confusing. What makes it confusing is that there is TRICARE North, South and West. That's not so bad BUT what makes it so confusing is that a different insurance company handles each of those geographic areas. Again you might say not so bad…. it still may sound simple but let me tell you. It isn't.

One issue is that Tricare changes contracts periodically which means it changes the insurance companies that handle our clients. That means each time the contract changes hands we have to be credentialed with the new company. In addition the website changes, the forms change, where claims are submitted changes, and all phone contact numbers change…. that means a big hot mess until everyone gets it together.

We have gone through one of those contract changes. When I began doing insurance billing for Dr. Julie TRICARE West was handled by TRIWEST. We or should I say I was very very happy with TRIWEST insurance company services. They had a phenomenal website that made it easy to submit claims. The people I dealt with on the phone were amazing. Then it all changed.

It all began with United Behavioral Health. This was the company that got the new contract with Tricare West. Dr. Julie had to be credentialed through them. There was no grandfathering in of providers. AND she had to go through a company called OPTUM to be credentialed. Then she found out that she was only credentialed with TRICARE not with United Behavioral Health even though they were the company doing the credentialing.

We kept wondering what the heck OPTUM was, where did they come from and what was their relationship to UBH. I only recently found out that OPTUM is United Behavioral Health doing business under the name OPTUM.

Then we were referred to a website called: UnitedHealth Military and Veterans.com to apply for authorizations for treatment. We thought it would be similar to the last process where everything was done on one website.

Get this -- though we can obtain a precertification form we can't submit online claims at that website. We found out that we had to submit claims on TRICARE Express.com website. Now after all that there is no mention of United Behavioral Health Insurance anywhere, which is, as you will recall where all this started.

I still am not sure of the whole set up. Here is what I have been able to figure out. I made the diagram for those of us who are more visual.

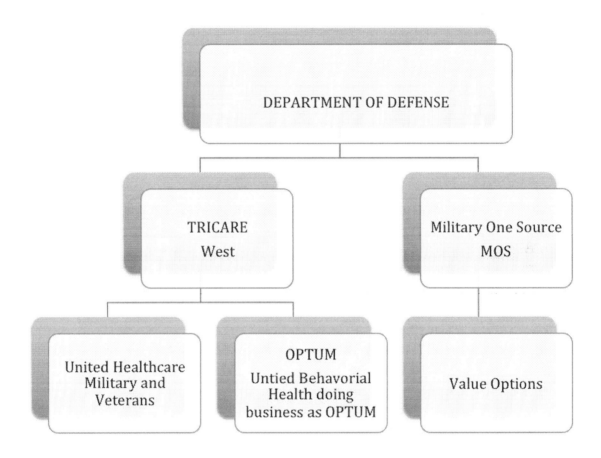

This chart might help reduce some of the confusion many of us feel when dealing with the military. If you are in a different region you can be prepared for a similar situation. We don't want to comment on the other regions because we don't have direct experience with them.

MOS Military One Source

As you see on the flowchart there is a service provided by the military called MOS, which is the acronym for Military One Source. This is a great service, which allows military personnel to seek mental health services privately to avoid potential stigma or consequences within the military system. Military One Source does not change from region to region. It is a service just as TRICARE is for military members, their families and veterans provided by the Department of Defense.

One might assume that MOS would also come under Tricare and UBH but one again would be so wrong. The MOS services are contracted with Value Options and that requires a totally different credentialing process and another website

So how does this work?

First Dr. Julie gets a call from MOS. The client is on the phone with them so she actually gets to interact with the client briefly. The MOS representative provides the service member's name and telephone number as well as type of service being requested and an authorization number.

A letter follows up this call from MOS repeating all aforementioned information. Usually the appointment is made during the phone call.

The MOS service provides for a limited number of visits after which, if more services are needed the client goes through a different process to obtain the extended treatment services.

MOS is different from Tricare in that, in order to bill for services, you must provide clinical notes for each session. This is done in an online format. It is surprisingly easy to use once you find the MOS section on the Value Options website. No not the UBH website or United HealthCare Military and Veterans.com nor Tricare North, South or West but Value Options.com

And Value Options has to credential you and you sign a contract with them. You have to register to use the website. But again, they call you and offer you clients. Oh and by the way you have to change your password every 120 days. Don't worry they remind you. Keep in mind that they refer clients to you.

CHAPTER 10 MEDICARE

Tips for the Mournful, Morose and Medicated

Medicare is surprisingly exclusive when it comes to who can provide services in the mental health arena. Only clinical social workers, clinical psychologists and regular old psychologists have the privilege of journeying down the rabbit hole of Medicare.

If you are a Marriage and Family Therapist you are out of luck or on the other hand unbelievably lucky because at the present time you do not qualify as provider for Medicare patients.

FYI as of August 2013 there is a bill going through Congress in an attempt to allow MFTs to provide behavioral health services to Medicare members. This bill has been a work in progress for a number of years so who knows when it will pass if ever. We suggest you just keep checking the status of the bill through your professional organization. Our national population is moving on in years and more people will be on Medicare.

What does it mean to participate in Medicare?

Participation requires you to accept assignment of claims for all services you furnish to Medicare beneficiaries. Translation: This means you agree to always accept Medicare-allowed amounts as payments in full and to not collect more than the Medicare deductible and coinsurance from the beneficiary.

So again you ask why are we doing this?

Here are the benefits:

First you get 5% more as a participant than a non-participating provider.

Second, the payments are issued directly to you because the claims are always assigned to the provider.

What the Heck does this all mean? Damned if we know.

So for those who are eligible to be a Medicare Provider, the first step is to register/enroll with Medicare. Yes I said with Medicare…directly. I say that because initially I was very confused about this process. I was working with an out-of-network provider and the insurance company kept saying she had to be registered and I thought they meant registered with the insurance company. I am embarrassed to say it took me awhile to get it. Actually I still don't get it.

There is an online enrollment process, which of course has an acronym, PECOS. This is short for Provider Enrollment, Chain and Ownership System. We are not making this up.

If you prefer the paper enrollment application process you have to locate and fill out a CMS 855. You can find this on the Medicare Enrollment site.

I will save you some time and heartache. When you see this acronym DMEPOS don't worry about it…this refers to durable medical suppliers, etc. and not to individual providers.

> ❖ TIP: If a Medicare patient has no supplemental insurance they have a $50 per visit copay. If they do have supplemental insurance they don't have the copay. Always verify this because it changes constantly.

Wish I had more information for you but to date we have not been involved with Medicare because Dr. Julie is licensed as a Marriage and Family Therapist. Remember at this time Medicare does not recognize MFTs.

> ❖ TIP: If you journey into the Medicare world they offer free courses on how to work with and bill Medicare. Go to the Medicare website.

CHAPTER 11 OUT OF THE RABBIT HOLE

Julie and I want to thank you for joining us on this trip through Insuranceland. Most likely you will find aspects of the world of behavioral health insurance as incomprehensible and impenetrable as we have. Not only was it difficult but when we looked for information pertinent to our field, it was not to be found. We had to learn through trial and error. We decided to make your experience easier by writing this damned book.

We have attempted to share with you our experiences and provide encouragement as you embark on your own journey. We think you will find that with this map you will be able to minimize some of the insanity as you do your own billing…until, of course, you can find your very own Dianne.

The insurance billing world is constantly changing; we have to keep up with that cwazy wabbit and stick together. You want to use all of your faculties to focus on your clients. They need you.

They will appreciate your ability to access their insurance. Hopefully our book has helped you to meet that need.

We know that this experience has made us a little cwazy and can just imagine what effect it would have on your clients if they had to do deal with their insurance companies.

We have covered every circumstance that we have so far encountered and blundered through. We know there are many more hurdles on the horizon for us. We are still relatively new to this madness and hope that you will share your own discoveries with us and with your peers. We invite you to go to our website www.mentalhealthinsurancebillingtips.com for new developments and new tips. In our next book we will continue with information on Medicare coverage, contracting with insurance companies and other topics we run into as we travel down the rabbit hole of Insuranceland.

In the mean time don't let the Mad Hatter get to you. Just remember to breathe.

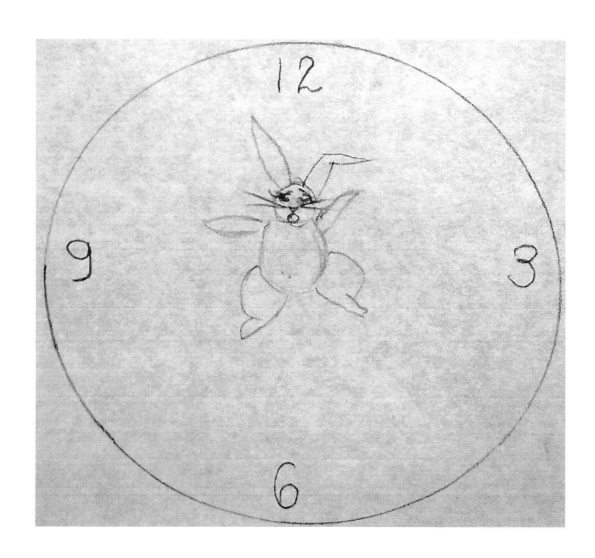

GLOSSARY

Accept Assignment – This term is found in block 27 on CMS 1500 form. When it is checked with "yes" it is permission from client to the insurance company to pay you directly vs. the insurance company paying the client directly. Don't forget to check the "yes" box.

ABA - Applied Behavioral Analysis, which is a form of treatment often used for Autism used to modify behavior. Often providers must go through a different process with the insurance company. Make sure this is covered by the patient's insurance.

Administrator - This is the insurance company that writes the policy.

Allowed Amount - Amount the insurance company will pay no matter what you have billed.

Annual Maximum - That's all folks. Total amount the patient is covered for in one calendar year for your services. This may change with the Affordable Health Act. So check it out.

Authorization Number - Goes in Box 23 on CMS 1500. (See Chapter 3.) Some insurance companies that require preauthorization or authorization for services provide this number. You may or may not have to insert number into CMS 1500.

CAQH - This is an acronym for Council for Affordable Quality Healthcare, which hosts a universal credentialing database for healthcare providers. Some insurance companies use this organization to credential you.

Carve-out - Is an arrangement in which some benefits, such as mental health, are provided through a contract with a separate insurance company.

Claim - To submit your invoice for services rendered you must use the CMS 1500 form.

Claim Scrubber - Software that makes sure all necessary information is on the form. This helps prevent an insurance company from returning your claim for corrections. When claims are returned for missing information it takes longer to get paid.

Clearinghouse - For our purposes this is an organization that will do the hard work for us and send the CMS1500 to the insurance companies. The clearinghouse provides the claim-scrubbing software as part of their services.

Coinsurance - Refers to client's insurance. Both client and insurance company share cost of covered services after the deductible has been met. Client pays a percentage of the amount that is contracted for in network provider

Copay - Amount of money the client pays you at time of service as their portion of your fee. This is different from coinsurance because it is a set amount vs coinsurance which is a percentage of the allowed amount.

CPT - This is the acronym for Current Procedural Terminology. CPT codes are maintained and copyrighted by the American Medical Association. There is a number for each type of service provided. These numbers are required by insurer to determine the amount of reimbursement that practitioner will receive by an insurer. These are different from the DSM codes used for diagnosis.

Credentialing - Insurance companies' process of obtaining and verifying information to determine whether a behavioral heath provider meets required qualifications to provide services. This process can be different depending on the organization doing the credentialing.

EAP - This is the acronym for Employee Assistance Program. This is a service offered by companies to provide short-term treatment for an employee who may be having problems. The number of office visits is limited and referrals to longer-term treatment are an option.

EOB - This is the acronym for Explanation of Benefits. This is the document produced each time services are submitted to a claims administrator and mailed to you. Please note you may not collect the difference between your charged amount and the maximum allowable from the client.

HIPPA - This is the acronym for the Health Insurance Portability and Accountability Act. For further details and information we refer you to the website http: //www.hhs.gov/ocr/privacy/hipaa/understanding/summary/.

HMO - This is the acronym for Health Management Organization. HMOs are organizations that offer health care coverage with contracted providers. It differs from traditional heath insurance because of the contracts it has with its providers. These contracts pay lower premiums because the provider has the advantage of having patients directed to him/her.

In-network provider - An in network provider has met the criteria of the insurance company and has signed a contract with the insurer

Network – A network is made up of a group of health care professionals who have been approved by and are contracted with an insurance health plan to provide mental health care services.

Out-of-network provider - This refers to providers who do not belong to a network. Some plans provide coverage for services received from out of network professionals.

Panel - For insurance companies that utilize in-network providers a panel is simply the list of in-network providers.

PPO - Preferred provider organization. This is a specific type of health plan with a national network of providers. Clients can visit providers both in and out of network and can visit specialists without a referral. Annual deductible is usually required.

Reference Number - This is a number assigned to your phone call whenever you call the insurance company. It is important to ask for this number before you hang up because if you have to call back about the same issue just give them that number and they can look up all previous contact information.

Remittance Advice - Is a document supplied by the insurance payer that provides notice of and explanation reasons for payment, adjustment, denial and/or uncovered charges of a medical claim.

NEW VERSION CMS 1500

ALL THE TIPS

- **TIP**: When filling out your information online be sure to use the back button on the web page vs. your browser back button …I didn't and had to laboriously fill in the information all over again. And again. And so forth.

- **TIP**: If you have a specialty, flaunt it. Make sure to emphasize your training and experience.

- **TIP**: To avoid this eventuality you will have to stay on top of them. (No we didn't mean THAT! Just making sure you're awake.) So it is worth the time to mark your calendar to periodically call and check on your application

- **TIP**: Get your smart phone out and set an alarm to follow up and ensure they received the initial packet. I suggest you call every few weeks and ask if there are any problems.

- TIP: MAKE A COPY OF THE INSURANCE CARD FRONT AND BACK TO HAVE ON FILE. Make sure you can read the copy. If the client's name on the CMS 1500 is not spelled exactly as it is written on the card or if the number is wrong you have just wasted a lot of time.

- TIP: Even though insurance companies have the demographic data on the client, according to HIPPA, sending in a claim equals our sending private information about the client to an outside source. Hence, you better be sure to have them sign Blocks 12 and 13 and keep it on file.

- TIP: Diagnosis codes: I have found that one can -- Google codes. If you don't want to scan through that huge DSM-V…. just Google it. The world according to Google is amazing.

- TIP: Check it out: Some insurance companies do not accept V codes. Some insurance companies don't pay for sexual disorder diagnoses. And then there are those that <u>only</u> accept V Codes. Confused? Join the club. You need to call and ask.

- TIP: To find the latest CPT codes go to www.ama-assn.org/go/cpt.

- TIP: Beginning in 2014 a new CMS 1500 will be in use. Please check the website for details. www.nucc.org. Basically the same form with minimal changes.

- TIP: ALWAYS make a copy of the claim you are submitting. I repeat always make a copy of the claim. Often there is a link that says PRINT. Other times I just do a print screen....if there's a glitch, you have proof!

- TIP: First thing to do when you call is to ASK FOR HELP.

- Remember to sound needy.

- I will remind you of this because it is critical to your peace of mind and increases the chance you will get helped.

- TIP: When calling insurance companies make sure you DOCUMENT, DOCUMENT, and oh don't forget to DOCUMENT!

- TIP: Remember to breathe deeply, relax and be prepared to be on the phone for a while. I guarantee if you get the answers to your questions in your first contact you are saving yourself time, sweat, tears and most important saving $$.

- TIP: You can NEVER EVER use standard email to send client information as per HIPPA regulations.

- **TIP:** Make a note on your calendar when the number of sessions is close to being completed or the time limit is near. Call to find out what to do to receive approval for more visits. Do this in a timely manner. Ask how long the approval process takes. You don't want to wait for them to mail you the paperwork. It takes forever.

- Ask for the phone number to call after the paperwork is submitted to verify approval. Make sure you ask for the right number to call. Yes, yes, yet another number. You can never go wrong asking for the specific phone number. Sigh!

- TIP: Usually it is a simple fix and all you have to do is resubmit whatever you forgot -- see if you can fax it for quickest results. Ask what the subject line should be and to whom should it be addressed. Be sure to verify the fax number. Even if you have it -- VERIFY. They change numbers. Also ask for a reference number for this call.

- ❖ TIP: Don't just accept the denial....call and ask WTF....but remember to ask the question with a really *good* attitude.

- ❖ **TIP**: Do not accept or agree to any reduction in payment. You don't have to and they can't make you. So there!

- ❖ TIP: This will save you time when you have to call the company again. As time goes on you will have multiple numbers for multiple companies and it gets confusing to keep it all straight

- ❖ TIP: And as a matter of fact the financial information is not supposed to be kept with the clinical record.

- ❖ TIP: Knowing what I know now, I suppose a crafty therapist could call the insurance companies and inquire about their EAP programs. Why wait?

- ❖ TIP: If a Medicare patient has no supplemental insurance they have a $50 per visit copay. If they do have supplemental insurance they don't have the copay. Always verify this because it changes constantly.

- ❖ TIP: If you journey into the Medicare world they offer free courses on how to work with and bill Medicare. Go to the Medicare website.

BIBLIOGRAPHY

Frager, S. (2000). *Managing Managed Care.* New York:John Wiley&Sons.

Griswold, B. (2014). *Navigating the Insurance Maze.* (Fifth edition, p. 42) San Jose, CA: Paper Street Press.

Scott, A & Redmond, A (2011). *Mental Health Billing Made Easy.* Kentucky:Solutions Medical Billing.

RESOURCES

CMS 1500 - New form information www.nucc.org

Susan Frager, LCSW, Billing Specialist www.psychadminpartners.com

Our Website: www.mentalhealthinsurancebillingtips.com

Barbara Griswold, LMFT Consultant www.theInsuranceMaze.com

ILLUSTRATIONS

❖ Wabbits..Courtesy of Julie A Rice, PsyD, LMFT, 2014

Made in the USA
Lexington, KY
31 March 2015